C000066894

THE *156*

SORCERER.

AN ENTIRELY ORIGINAL

MODERN COMIC OPERA,

IN TWO ACTS.

WRITTEN BY W. S. GILBERT.
COMPOSED BY Sir ARTHUR Seymour SULLIVAN.

NEW YORK:
A. S. SEER. PRINTER,
26 UNION SQUARE (Fourth Avc. and 15th St.)
1879.

Music
ML
50
.S95
S7
1879

DRAMATIS PERSONÆ.

SIR MARMADUKE POINTDEXTRE, an elderly Baronet.

ALEXIS, of the Grenadier Guards, his son.

DR. DALY, Vicar of Ploverleigh.

NOTARY.

JOHX WELLINGTON WELLS, of J. Wells & Co., Family Sorcerers.

LADY SANGAZURE, of Ancient Lineage.

ALINE, her daughter—betrothed to Alexis.

MRS. PARTLET, a pew opener.

CONSTANCE, her daughter.

Chorus of Peasantry.

Samuel J. Bigelow
3-26-42

THE SORCERER.

ACT I.

SCENE.—*Garden of Sir Marmaduke's Elizabethan mansion. The end of a large marquee, open, and showing portion of table covered with white cloth, on which are joints of meat, teapots, cups, bread and butter, jam, etc. Across the back of the stage a raised terrace. A park in the background, with spire of church seen above the trees.*

CHORUS OF PEASANTRY.

Ring forth, ye bells,
　With clarion sound,
Forget your knells,
　For joys abound ;
Forget your notes
　Of mournful lay,
And from your throats
　Pour joy to-day.

For to-day young Alexis—young Alexis Pointdextre
　Is betrothed to Aline—to Aline Sangazure,
And that pride of his sex is—of his sex is to be next her
　At the feast on the green—on the green ; oh, be sure !
　　Ring forth, ye bells, etc.
　　　　　　　　(*Exeunt the men into house.*)

Enter Mrs. PARTLET, *meeting* CONSTANCE, *her daughter.*

RECITATIVE.

MRS. P.　Constance, my daughter, why this strange depression ?
　　　　The village rings with seasonable joy,
　　　　Because the young and amiable Alexis,
　　　　Heir to the great Sir Marmaduke Pointdextre,
　　　　Is plighted to Aline, the only daughter
　　　　Of Annabella, Lady Sangazure.
　　　　You, you alone, are sad and out of spirits ;
　　　　What is the reason ?　Speak, my daughter, speak !
CON.　　O mother, do not ask !　If my complexion
　　　　From red to white should change in quick succession,
　　　　And then from white to red, oh, take no notice !
　　　　If my poor limbs shall tremble with emotion,
　　　　Pay no attention, mother—it is nothing !

If long and deep drawn sighs I chance to utter,
Oh, heed them not—their cause must ne'er be known !

MRS. P. My child, be candid. Think not to deceive
The eagle-eyed pew-opener—you love !

CON. (*aside.*) How guessed she that, my heart's most cher-
ished secret ?
(*aloud.*) I *do* love—fondly—madly—hopelessly !

ARIA,—CONSTANCE.

When he is here,
I sigh with pleasure ;
When he is gone,
I sigh with grief ;
My hopeless fear
No soul can measure,
His love alone
Can give my aching heart relief !
When he is cold,
I weep for sorrow;
When he is kind,
I weep for joy ;
My grief untold
Knows no to-morrow,
My woe can find
No hope, no solace, no alloy !

MRS. PARTLET *silently motions to women to leave them together.*
Exeunt chorus.

MRS. P. Come, tell me all about it ! Do not fear.
I, too, have loved, but that was long ago.
Who is the object of your young affections ?

CON. Hush, mother ! He is here !

Enter DR. DALY. *He is pensive and does not see them.*

MRS. P. Our reverend vicar !
CON. Oh pity me, my heart is almost broken !
MRS. P. My child, be comforted. To such an union
I shall not offer any opposition.
Take him—he's yours ! May you and he be happy !
CON. But, mother, dear, he is not yours to give.
MRS. P. That's true, indeed.
CON. He might object.
MRS. P. He might.
But come, take heart, I'll probe him on the subject.
Be comforted,—leave this affair to me.

RECITATIVE.—DR. DALY.

The air is charged with amatory numbers—
Soft madrigals and dreamy lovers' lays.
Peace, peace, old heart ! Why waken from its slumbers
The aching memory of the old, old days ?

BALLAD.

Time was when love and I were well acquainted;
　Time was when we walked ever hand in hand;
A saintly youth, with wordly thought untainted,
　None better loved than I in all the land!
Time was when maidens of the noblest station,
　Forsaking even military men,
Would gaze upon me, rapt in adoration,—
　Ah me, I was a fair young curate then!

Had I a headache? sighed the maids assembled;
　Had I a cold? welled forth the silent tear;
Did I look pale? then half a parish trembled;
　And when I coughed all thought the end was near.
I had no care, no jealous doubts hung o'er me,
　For I was loved beyond all other men;
Fled gilded dukes and belted earls before me,—
　Ah me, I was a pale young curate then!

MRS. PARTLET *comes forward with* CONSTANCE.

MRS. P. Good day, reverend sir.

DR. D. Ah, good Mrs. Partlet, I am glad to see you. And your little daughter, Constance—why, she is quite a little woman, I declare!

CON. (*aside.*) O mother, I cannot speak to him!

MRS. P. Yes, reverend sir, she is nearly eighteen, and as good a girl as ever stepped. (*Aside to* DR. D.) Ah, sir, I'm afraid I shall soon lose her!

DR. D. (*aside to* MRS. P.) Dear me, you pain me very much. Is she delicate?

MRS. P. Oh, no, sir, I don't mean that; but young girls look to get married.

DR. D. Oh, I take you. To be sure. But there's plenty of time for that. Four or five years hence, Mrs. Partlet, four or five years hence. But when the time *does* come, I shall have much pleasure in marrying her myself—

CON. (*aside.*) Oh, mother!

DR. D. To some strapping young fellow in her own rank of life.

CON. He does *not* love me!

MRS. P. I have often wondered, reverend sir (if you'll excuse the liberty), that *you* have never married.

DR. D. (*aside.*) Be still, my fluttering heart!

MRS. P. A clergyman's wife does so much good in a village. Besides that, you are not so young as you were, and before very long you will want some one to nurse you, and look after your little comforts.

DR. D. Mrs. Partlet, there is much truth in what you say. I am indeed getting on in years, and a helpmate would cheer my declining days. Time was when it might have been, but I have left it too long. I am an old fogy now, am I not, my dear? (*to* CONSTANCE)—a very old fogy indeed. Ha, ha! No, Mrs. Partlet, my mind is quite made up. I shall live and die a solitary old bachelor.

Con. Oh mother, mother !

Mrs. P. Come, come, dear one, don't fret. At a more fitting time we will try again—we will try again.

(*Exeunt* Mrs. Partlet *and* Constance.)

Dr. D. (*looking after them.*) Poor little girl ! I'm afraid she has something on her mind. She is rather comely. Time was when this old heart would have throbbed in double-time at the sight of such a fairy form ! But tush ! I am puling ! Here comes the young Alexis, with his proud and happy father. Let me dry this tell-tale tear !

Enter Sir Marmaduke *and* Alexis *from house.*

Recitative.

Dr. D. Sir Marmaduke—my dear young friend, Alexis—
On this most happy, most auspicious plighting,
Permit me, as a true old friend, to tender
My best, my very best congratulations !

Sir M. Sir, you are most obleeging !

Alexis.   Dr. Daly,
My dear old tutor and my valued pastor,
I thank you from the bottom of my heart!

Dr. D. May fortune bless you ! may the middle distance
Of your young life be pleasant as the foreground—
The joyous foreground ! and, when you have reached it,
May that which now is the far-off horizon,
But which will then become the middle distance,
In fruitful promise be exceeded only
By that which will have opened, in the mean time,
Into a new and glorious horizon !

(Alexis *sits on stool.*)

Sir M. Dear sir, that is an excellent example
Of an old school of stately compliment
To which I have, through life, been much addicted.
Will you obleege me with a copy of it,
In clerkly manuscript, that I myself
May use it on appropriate occasions?

Dr. D. Sir, you shall have a fairly-written copy
Ere Sol has sunk into his western slumbers.

(*Exit* Dr. Daly.)

Sir M. (*to* Alexis.) Come, come, my son, your *fiancée* will be here in five minutes. Rouse yourself to receive her.

Alexis. (*rising.*) Oh, rapture !

Sir M. Yes, you are a fortunate young fellow, and I will not disguise from you that this union with the House of Sangazure realizes my fondest wishes. Aline is rich, and she comes of a sufficiently old family, for she is the seven thousand and thirty-seventh in direct descent from Helen of Troy. True, there was a blot on the escutcheon of that lady—that affair with Paris—but where is the family, other than my own, in which there is no flaw? You are a lucky fellow, sir—a very lucky fellow !

ALEXIS. Father, I am welling over with limpid joy! No sicklying taint of sorrow overlies the lucid lake of liquid love upon which, hand in hand, Aline and I are to float into eternity!

SIR M. Alexis, I desire that of your love for this young lady you do not speak so openly. You are always singing ballads in praise of her beauty, and you expect the very menials who wait behind your chair to chorus your ecstasies. It is not delicate.

ALEXIS. Father, a man who loves as I love—

SIR M. Pooh, pooh, sir! fifty years ago I madly loved your future mother-in-law, the Lady Sangazure, and I have reason to believe that she returned my love. But were we guilty of the indelicacy of publicly rushing into each other's arms, exclaiming:

RECITATIVE.

"Oh, my adored one!" "Beloved boy!"
"Ecstatic rapture!" "Unmingled joy!"

which seems to be the modern fashion of love-making? No! it was, "Madam, I trust you are in the enjoyment of good health." "Sir, you are vastly polite; I protest I am mighty well," and so forth. Much more delicate, much more respectful. But see, Aline approaches. Let us retire, that she may compose herself for the interesting ceremony in which she is to play so important a part.

Exeunt SIR MARMADUKE *and* ALEXIS *into house. Enter* ALINE *on terrace, preceded by chorus of girls.*

CHORUS OF GIRLS.

With heart and with voice
  Let us welcome this mating.
To the youth of her choice,
  With a heart palpitating,
    Comes the lovely Aline!

May their love never cloy!
  May their bliss be unbounded!
With a halo of joy
  May their lives be surrounded!
    Heaven bless our Aline!

RECITATIVE.—ALINE.

My kindly friends, I thank you for this greeting,
And as you wish me every earthly joy,
I trust your wishes may have quick fulfilment!

ARIA.—ALINE.

O happy young heart,
  Comes thy young lord a-wooing,
With joy in his eyes,
  And pride in his breast!
Make much of thy prize,
  For he is the best
That ever came a-suing.

Yet—yet we must part,
   Young heart !
Yet—yet we must part !

O merry young heart,
 Bright are the days of thy wooing !
But happier far
 The days untried ;
No sorrow can mar,
 When Love has tied
The knot there's no undoing.
 Then never to part,
   Young heart !
 Then never to part !

Enter LADY SANGAZURE *on terrace.*

RECITATIVE.—LADY S.

My child, I join in these congratulations.
Heed not the tear that dims this aged eye.
Old memories crowd upon me.   Though I sorrow,
'Tis for myself, Aline, and not for thee !

Enter ALEXIS *from house, preceded by Chorus of Men.*

CHORUS OF MEN AND WOMEN.

With heart and with voice
 Let us welcome this mating.
To the maid of his choice,
 With a heart palpitating,
  Comes Alexis the brave !

SIR MARMADUKE *enters from house.* LADY SANGAZURE *and he exhibit signs of strong emotion at the sight of each other, which they endeavor to repress.* ALEXIS *and* ALINE *rush into each other's arms.*

RECITATIVE.

ALEXIS. Oh, my adored one !
ALINE.   Beloved boy !
ALEXIS. Ecstatic rapture !
ALINE.   Unmingled joy !

DUET.—SIR MARMADUKE *and* LADY SANGAZURE.

SIR M. Welcome joy, adieu to sadness !
   As Aurora gilds the day,
  So those eyes, twin orbs of gladness,
   Chase the clouds of care away.
  Irresistible incentive
   Bids me humbly kiss your hand.
  I'm your servant most attentive,
   Most attentive to command !

Wild with adoration,
Mad with fascination,
To indulge my lamentation
 No occasion do I miss ;
Goaded to distraction
By maddening inaction,
I find some satisfaction
 In apostrophe like this :
" Sangazure, immortal,
 Sangazure, divine,
Welcome to my portal,—
 Angel, oh, be mine !" .

Irresistible incentive
 Bids me humbly kiss your hand.
I'm your servant, most attentive,
 Most attentive to command !

LADY S. Sir, I thank you most politely
 For your graceful courtesy ;
Compliments more truly knightly
 Never yet was paid to me.
Chivalry is an ingredient
 Sadly lacking in our land.
Sir, I am your most obedient,
 Most obedient to command !

Wild with adoration,
Mad with fascination,
To indulge my lamentation
 No occasion do I miss !
Goaded to distraction
By maddening inaction,
I find some satisfaction
 In apostrophe like this :
" Marmaduke, immortal,
 Marmaduke, divine,
Take me to thy portal,—
 Loved one, oh, be mine !"

Chivalry is an ingredient
 Sadly lacking in our land.
Sir, I am your most obedient,
 Most obedient to command !

During this duet, a small table has been placed up stage by MRS.
PARTLET. *The* COUNSEL *has entered, and prepares marriage
contract.*

RECIT.—COUNSEL.

All is prepared for sealing and for signing,
 The contract has been drafted as agreed.
Approach the table, oh ye lovers pining,
 With hand and seal, come, execute the deed !

ALEXIS *and* ALINE *advance and sign,*—ALEXIS *supported by* SIR MARMADUKE, ALINE *by her mother.*

CHORUS.

See, they sign, without a quiver, it ;
Then to seal proceed.
They deliver it, they deliver it
As their act and deed !

ALEXIS. I deliver it, I deliver it
As my act and deed !
ALINE. I deliver it, I deliver it
As my act and deed !

CHORUS.

With heart and with voice
Let us welcome this mating,
Leave them here to rejoice,
With true love palpitating,—
Alexis the brave,
And the lovely Aline !
(*Exeunt all but* ALEXIS *and* ALINE.)

ALEXIS. At last we are alone ! My darling, you are now irrevocably betrothed to me. Are you not very, very happy ?

ALINE. O Alexis, can you doubt it ? Do I not love you beyond all on earth, and am I not beloved in return ? Is not true love, faithfully given and faithfully returned, the source of every earthly joy ?

ALEXIS. Of that there can be no doubt. Oh, that the world could be persuaded of the truth of that maxim ! Oh, that the world would break down the artificial barriers of rank, wealth, education, age, beauty, habits, taste, and temper, and recognize the glorious principle that in marriage alone is to be found the panacea for every ill.

ALINE. Continue to preach that sweet doctrine, and you will succeed, O evangel of true happiness !

ALEXIS. I hope so, but as yet the cause progresses but slowly. Still, I have made some converts to the principle that men and women should be coupled in matrimony without distinction of rank. I have lectured on the subject at Mechanics' Institute, and the mechanics were unanimous in favor of my views. I have preached in work-houses, beer-shops, and lunatic asylums, and I have been received with enthusiasm. I have addressed navvies on the advantages that would accrue to them if they married wealthy ladies of rank, and not a navvy dissented !

ALINE. Noble fellows ! And yet there are those who hold that the uneducated classes are not open to argument ! And what do the countesses say ?

ALEXIS. Why, at present, it can't be denied, the aristocracy hold aloof.

ALINE. The workingman is the true intelligence after all !

ALEXIS. He is a noble creature when he is quite sober. Yes, Aline, true happiness comes of true love, and true love should be independent of external influences. It should live upon itself and by itself ; in itself, love should live for love alone !

BALLAD.—ALEXIS.

Love feeds on many kinds of food, I know—
  Some love for rank, and some for duty ;
Some give their hearts away for empty show,
  And others love for youth and beauty.
To love for money all the world is prone ;
  Some love themselves, and live all lonely.
Give me the love that loves for love alone—
  I love that love, I love it only !

What man for any other joy can thirst,
  Whose loving wife adores him duly?
Want, misery, and care may do their worst,
  If loving woman loves you truly.
A lover's thoughts are ever with his own ;
  None truly loved is ever lonely.
Give me the love that loves for love alone—
  I love that love, I love it only !

ALINE. O Alexis, those are noble principles !

ALEXIS. Yes, Aline, and I am going to take a desperate step in support of them. Have you ever heard of the firm of J. W. Wells & Co., the old established Family Sorcerers, in St. Mary Axe ?

ALINE. I have seen their advertisement.

ALEXIS. They have invented a philter, which, if report may be believed, is simply infallible. I intend to distribute it through the village, and within half an hour of my doing so, there will not be an adult in the place who will not have learnt the secret of pure and lasting happiness. What do you say to that?

ALINE. Well, dear, of course a filter is a very useful thing in a house—quite indispensable in the present state of the Thames water ; but still I don't quite see that it is the sort of thing that places its possessor on the very pinnacle of earthly joy.

ALEXIS. Aline, you misunderstand me. I didn't say a filter—I said philter.

ALINE. So did I, dear. *I* said a filter.

ALEXIS. No, dear, you said a filter. I don't mean a filter—I mean a philter—ph, you know.

ALINE. You don't mean a love-potion ?

ALEXIS. On the contrary, I *do* mean a love-potion.

ALINE. O Alexis, I don't think it would be right ; I don't indeed. And then—a real magician ! Oh, it would be downright wicked !

ALEXIS. Aline, is it, or is it not, a laudable object to steep the whole village up to its lips in love, and to couple them in matrimony without distinction of age, rank, or fortune ?

ALINE. Unquestionably, but—

ALEXIS. Then, unpleasant as it must be to have recourse to supernatural aid, I must nevertheless pocket my aversion, in deference to the great and good end I have in view. Hercules !

Enter a Page from tent.

PAGE. Yes, sir.

ALEXIS. Is Mr. Wells there?

PAGE. He's in the tent, sir—refreshing.

ALEXIS. Ask him to be so good as to step this way.

PAGE. Yes, sir. *(Exit Page.)*

ALINE. Oh, but Alexis! A real Sorcerer! Oh, I shall be frightened to death!

ALEXIS. I trust my Aline will not yield to fear while the strong right arm of her Alexis is here to protect her.

ALINE. It's nonsense, dear, to talk of your protecting me with your strong right arm, in face of the fact that this Family Sorcerer could change me into a guinea-pig before you could turn round.

ALEXIS. He *could* change you into a guinea-big, no doubt, but it is most unlikely that he would take such a liberty. It's a most respectable firm, and I am sure he would never be guilty of so untradesmanlike an act.

Enter MR. WELLS from tent.

MR. W. Good day, sir.

ALEXIS. Good day; I believe you are a Sorcerer.

MR. W. Yes, sir; we practise Necromancy in all its branches. We've a choice assortment of wishing-caps, divining-rods, amulets, charms, and counter-charms. We can cast you a nativity at a low figure, and we have a horoscope at three-and-six that we can guarantee. Our Abudah chests, each containing a patent Hag who comes out and prophesies disasters, with spring complete, are strongly recommended. Our Aladdin Lamps are very chaste, and our Prophetic Tablets, foretelling everything, from a change of Ministry down to a rise in Turkish Stock, are much inquired for. Our penny Curse, one of the cheapest things in the trade, is considered infallible. We have some very superior Blessings, too, but they're very little asked for. We've only sold one since Christmas, to a gentleman who bought it to send to his mother-in-law; but it turned out that he was afflicted in the head, and it's been returned on our hands. But our sale of penny Curses, especially on Saturday nights, is tremendous. We can't turn 'em out fast enough.

SONG.—MR. WELLS.

Oh! my name is John Wellington Wells,
I'm a dealer in magic and spells,
    In blessings and curses,
    And ever-filled purses,
In prophecies, witches, and knells.

If you want a proud foe to "make tracks,"
If you'd melt a rich uncle in wax,
    You've but to look in
    On our resident Djinn,
Number seventy, Simmery Axe.

We've a first-class assortment of magic;
    And for raising a posthumous shade
With effects that are comic or tragic,
    There's no cheaper house in the trade.

Love-philter—we've quantities of it !
And for knowledge, if any one burns,
We keep an extremely small prophet
Who brings us unbounded returns :

Oh ! he can prophecy
With a wink *of* his eye,
Peep with security
Into futurity,
Sum up your history,
Clear up a mystery,
Humor proclivity
For a nativity—for a nativity !
Mirrors so magical,
Tetrapods tragical,
Bogies spectacular,
Answers oracular.
Facts astronomical,
Solemn or comical.
And, if you want it, he
Makes a reduction on taking a quantity !
   Oh !
If any one anything lacks,
He'll find it all ready in stacks,
  If he'll only look in
  On the resident Djinn,
Number seventy, Simmery Axe !

He can raise you hosts
   Of ghosts,
And that, without reflectors ;
 And creepy things
   With wings,
And gaunt and grisly spectres ;
 He can fill you crowds
   Of shrouds,
And horrify you vastly ;
 He can rack your brains
   With chains,
And gibberings grim and ghastly !

Then, if you plan it, he
Changes organity
With an urbanity
Full of Satanity,
Vexes humanity
With an inanity
Fatal to vanity.
Driving your foes to the verge of insanity !
Barring tautology,
In demonology,
'Lectro biology,
Mystic nosology,
Spirit philology,
High-class astrology,

Such is his knowledge, he
Isn't the man to require an apology !
Oh !
My name is John Wellington Wells,
I'm a dealer in magic and spells,
In blessings and curses,
And ever filled purses,
In prophecies, witches, and knells.

If any one anything lacks,
He'll find it all ready in stacks,
If he'll only look in
On the resident Djinn,
Number seventy, Simmery Axe !

ALEXIS. I have sent for you to consult you on a very important
matter. I believe you advertise a Patent Oxy-Hydrogen Love-at-
first-sight Philter ?

MR. W. Sir, it is our leading article. (*Producing a phial.*)

ALEXIS. Now I want to know if you can confidently guarantee
it as possessing all the qualities you claim for it in your advertisement ?

MR. W. Sir, we are not in the habit of puffing our goods. Ours
is an old established house with a large family connection, and
every assurance held out in the advertisement is fully realized.

ALINE. (*aside.*) O Alexis, don't offend him ! He'll change us
into something dreadful—I know he will !

ALEXIS. I am anxious from purely philanthropical motives to
distribute this philter, secretly, among the inhabitants of this
village. I shall, of course, require a quantity. How do you
sell it ?

MR. W. In buying a quantity, sir, we should strongly advise
your taking it in the wood, and drawing it off as you happen to
want it. We have it in four and a half and nine gallon casks, also
in pipes and hogsheads for laying down, and we deduct ten per
cent. for prompt cash.

ALINE. O Alexis, surely you don't want to lay any down !

ALEXIS. Aline, the villagers will assemble to carouse in a few
minutes. Go and fetch the teapot.

ALINE. But, Alexis—

ALEXIS. My dear, you must obey me, if you please. Go and
fetch the teapot.

ALINE. I'm sure Dr. Daly would disapprove of it.

(*Exit* ALINE *into tent.*)

ALEXIS. And how soon does it take effect ?

MR. W. In half an hour. Whoever drinks of it falls in love,
as a matter of course, with the first lady he meets who has also
tasted it, and his affection is at once returned. One trial will
prove the fact. (*Enter* ALINE *from tent with large teapot.*)

ALEXIS. Good ! Then, Mr. Wells, I shall feel obliged if you
will at once pour as much philter into this teapot as will suffice to
affect the whole village.

ALINE. But, bless me, Alexis, many of the villagers are married
people.

MR. W. Madam, this philter is compounded on the strictest principles. On married people it has no effect whatever. But are you quite sure that you have nerve enough to carry you through the fearful ordeal?

ALEXIS. In the good cause, I fear nothing.

MR. W. Very good; then we will proceed at once to the Incantation.

INCANTATION.

MR. W.
> Sprites of earth and air,
>> Fiends of flame and fire,
>> Demon souls,
>> Come here ill shoals,
>> This dreadful deed inspire!
>> Appear, appear, appear!

MALE VOICES.
>> Good master, we are here!

MR. W.
> Noisome hags of night,
>> Imps of deadly shade,
>> Pallid ghosts
>> Arise in hosts
>> And lend me all your aid.
>> Appear, appear, appear!

FEMALE VOICES.
>> Good master, we are here!

ALEXIS. (*aside*.)
> Hark, they assemble,
>> These fiends of the night!

ALINE. (*aside*.)
> O Alexis, I tremble;
>> Seek safety in flight!

ARIA. —ALINE.

> Let us fly to a far-off land
>> Where peace and plenty dwell,
> Where the sigh of the silver strand
>> Is echoed in every shell;
> To the joy that land will give,
>> On the wings of Love we'll fly,
> In innocence there to live,
>> In innocence there to die!

CHORUS OF SPIRITS.

> Too late, too late!
> It may not be!
> That happy fate
> Is not for thee!

ALEXIS, ALINE *and* MR. WELLS.

> Too late, too late!
> That may not be!
> That happy fate
> Is not for { me!
> { thee!

MR. WELLS.

Now, shrivelled hags, with poison bags,
　　Discharge your loathsome loads!
Spit flame and fire, unholy choir!
　　Belch forth your venom, toads!
Ye demons fell, with yelp and yell,
　　Shed curses far a-field!
Ye fiends of night, your filthy blight
　　In noisome plenty yield!

MR. WELLS, (*pouring phial into teapot.*)

	Number One!
CHORUS.	It is done!
MR. W.	Number Two!
CHORUS.	One too few!
MR. W.	Number Three!
CHORUS.	Set us free!

Set us free. Our work is done!
　　Ha! ha! ha!
Set us free. Our course is run!
　　Ha! ha! ha!

ALINE *and* ALEXIS (*aside*).

Let us fly to a far-off land,
　　Where peace and plenty dwell;
Where the sigh of the silver strand
　　Is echoed in every shell.

CHORUS OF FIENDS.

Ha! ha! ha! ha! ha! ha! ha! ha! ha! ha!

Stage grows light. MR. WELLS *beckons villagers. Enter villagers, dancing joyously.* SIR MARMADUKE *enters with* LADY SANGAZURE *from house.* VICAR *enters on a terrace. He is followed by* CONSTANCE. COUNSEL *enters on terrace and down, followed by* MRS. PARTLET. MRS. PARTLET *and* MR. WELLS *distribute teacups.*

CHORUS.

Now to the banquet we press!
　　Now for the eggs, the ham,
Now for the mustard and cress,
　　Now for the strawberry jam!
Now for the tea of our host,
　　Now for the rollicking bun,
Now for the muffin and toast,
　　Now for the gay Sally Lunn!

WOMEN.	The eggs and the ham and the strawberry jam!
MEN.	The rollicking bun and the gay Sally Lunn!
	The rollicking, rollicking bun!

RECIT.—SIR MARMADUKE.

Be happy all ! The feast is spread before ye ;
  Fear nothing, but enjoy yourselves, I pray !
Eat, ay, and drink ; be merry, I implore ye ;
  For once, let thoughtless Folly rule the day !

TEACUP BRINDISI.

Eat, drink, and be gay,
  Banish all worry and sorrow !
Laugh gayly to-day,
  Weep, if you're sorry to-morrow !
Come, pass the cup round,
  I will go bail for the liquor ;
It's strong, I'll be bound,
  For it was brewed by the vicar !

CHORUS.

None so knowing as he
At brewing a jorum of tea,—
  Ha ! ha !
A pretty stiff jorum of tea !

TRIO.—MR. WELLS, ALINE *and* ALEXIS. (*Aside.*)

See, see ! they drink,
  All thought unheeding ;
The teacups clink,
  They are exceeding !
Their hearts will melt
  In half an hour ;
Then will be felt
  The potion's power !

During this verse, CONSTANCE *has brought a small teapot, kettle, caddy, and cosy to* DR. DALY.

BRINDISI, 2d *Verse.*—DR. DALY (*with the teapot*).

Pain, trouble, and care,
  Misery, heart-ache, and worry,
Quick, out of your lair !
  Get you all gone in a hurry !
Toil, sorrow, and plot
  Fly away quicker and quicker.
Three spoons to the pot,—
  That is the brew of your vicar !

CHORUS.

None so cunning as he
At brewing a jorum of tea,—
  Ha ! ha !
A pretty stiff joram of tea !

CHORUS.   You're everything that girls detest,
          But still she loves you dearly !

NOTARY.   I caught that line, but for the rest
          I did not hear it-clearly !

During this verse ALINE *and* ALEXIS *have entered at back unobserved.*

ALINE *and* ALEXIS.

ALEXIS.   Oh, joy ! oh, joy !
          The charm works well,
            And all are now united.

ALINE.   The blind young boy
          Obeys the spell,
            The troth they all have plighted !

ENSEMBLE.

ALINE *and* ALEXIS.	CONSTANCE.	NOTARY.
Oh, joy ! oh, joy ! The charm works well, And all are now united !	Oh, bitter joy ! No words can tell How my poor heart is blighted !	Oh, joy ! oh, joy ! No words can tell My state of mind de-lighted.
The blind young boy Obeys the spell, Their troth they all have plighted.	They'll soon employ A marriage bell, To say that we're united !	They'll soon employ A marriage bell To say that we're uni-ted !
True happiness Reigns everywhere, And dwells with both the sexes ;	I do confess A sorrow rare My humbled spirit vexes,	True happiness Reigns everywhere, And dwells with both the sexes,
And all will bless The thoughtful care Of their beloved Alexis !	And none will bless Example rare Of their beloved Alexis!	And all will bless Example rare Of their beloved Alexis !

All, except ALEXIS *and* ALINE, *dance off to symphony.*

ALINE.   How joyful they all seem in their new-found happiness ! The whole village has paired off in the happiest manner. And yet not a match has been made that the hollow world would not consider ill-advised !

ALEXIS.   But we are wiser, far wiser than the world. Observe the good that will become of these ill-assorted unions ! The miserly wife will check the reckless expenditure of her too frivolous consort ; the wealthy husband will shower innumerable bonnets on his penniless bride : and the young and lively spouse will cheer the declining days of her aged partner with comic songs unceasing.

ALINE.   What a delightful prospect for him !

ALEXIS.   But one thing remains to be done, that my happiness may be complete. We must drink the philter ourselves, that I may be assured of your love for ever and ever.

ALINE.   O Alexis, do you doubt me ? Is it necessary that such love as ours should be secured by artificial means ? Oh, no, no, no !

ALEXIS.   My dear Aline, time works terrible changes, and I want to place our love beyond the chance of change.

ALINE.   Alexis, it is already far beyond that chance. Have faith in me, for my love can never, never change.

ALEXIS.   Then you absolutely refuse ?

ALINE.   I do. If you cannot trust me, you have no right to love me,—no right to be loved *by* me.

ALEXIS. Enough, Aline, I shall know how to interpret this re-fusal.

BALLAD.—ALEXIS.

Thou hast the power thy vaunted love
To sanctify, all doubt above,
 Despite the gathering shade,
To make that love of thine so sure
That, come what may, it must endure
 Till time itself shall fade.
  Thy love is but a flower
  That fades within the hour.
  If such thy love, oh, shame !
  Call it by other name,—
   It is not love.

Thine is the power, and thine alone,
To place me on so proud a throne
 That kings might envy me,—
A priceless throne of love untold,
More rare than orient pearl and gold.
  But no, thou wouldst be free !
  Such love is like the ray
  That dies within the day.
  If such thy love, oh, shame !
  Call it by other name,—
   It is not love.   (*They retire.*)

Enter DR. DALY.

DR. D. It is singular, it is very singular. It has overthrown all my calculations. It is distinctly opposed to the doctrine of averages. I cannot understand it.

ALINE. Dear Dr. Daly, what has puzzled you?

DR. D. My dear, this village has not, hitherto, been addicted to marrying and given in marriage. Hitherto the youths of this village have not been enterprising, and the maidens have been distinctly coy. Judge, then, of my surprise when I tell you that the whole village came to me in a body just now, and implored me to join them in matrimony with as little delay as possible. Even your excellent father has hinted to me that before very long it is not unlikely that he, also, may change his condition.

ALINE. O Alexis, do you hear that? Are you not delighted?

ALEXIS. Yes. I confess that a union between your mother and my father would be a happy circumstance indeed. My dear sir, the news that you bring us is very gratifying.

DR. D. Yes; still, in my eyes, it has its melancholy side. This universal marrying recalls the happy days—now, alas, gone for-ever!—when I myself might have—but tush ! I am puling. I am too old to marry ; and yet, within the last half-hour, I have greatly yearned for companionship. I never remarked it before, but the young maidens of this village are very comely. So likewise are the middle-aged. Also the elderly. All are comely, and—all are engaged !

ALINE. Here comes your father.

Enter SIR MARMADUKE *with* MRS. PARTLET.

ALINE *and* ALEXIS. (*aside.*) Mrs. Partlet!

SIR M. Dr. Daly, give me joy! Alexis, my dear boy, you will, I am sure, be pleased to hear that my declining days are not unlikely to be solaced by the companionship of this good, virtuous, and amiable woman.

ALEXIS. My dear father, this is not altogether what I expected. I am certainly taken somewhat by surprise. Still, it can hardly be necessary to assure you that any wife of yours is a mother of mine. (*Aside to* ALINE) It is not quite what I could have wished.

MRS. P. O sir, I entreat your forgiveness. I am aware that socially I am not everything that could be desired, nor am I blessed with an abundance of worldly goods, but I can at least confer on your estimable father the great and priceless dowry of a true, tender, and loving heart.

ALEXIS. I do not question it. After all, a faithful love is the true source of every earthly joy.

SIR M. I knew that my boy would not blame his poor father for acting on the impulse of a heart that has never yet misled him. Zorah is not perhaps what the world calls beautiful—

DR. D. Still she is comely, distinctly comely!

ALINE. Zorah is very good, and very clean and honest, and quite, quite sober in her habits, and that is worth far more than beauty, dear Sir Marmaduke.

DR. D. Yes, beauty will fade and perish, but personal cleanliness is practically undying, for it can be renewed whenever it discovers symptoms of decay. My dear Sir Marmaduke, I heartily congratulate you.

QUINTETTE.

ALEXIS, ALINE, SIR MARMADUKE, ZORAH, *and* DR. DALY.

ALEXIS. I rejoice that it is decided ;
    Happy now will be his life ;
For my father is provided
    With a true and tender wife.

ENSEMBLE. She will tend him, nurse him, mend him ;
    Air his linen, dry his tears.
Bless the thoughtful fates that send him
    Such a wife to soothe his years !

ALINE. No young, giddy, thoughtless maiden,
    Full of graces, airs, and jeers,
But a sober widow, laden
    With the weight of fifty years !

SIR M. No high-born, exacting beauty,
    Blazing like a jeweled sun,
But a wife, who'll do her duty
    As that duty should be done !

MRS. P. I'm no saucy minx and giddy,
    Hussies such as they abound,
But a clean and tidy widdy,
    Well beknown for miles around !

Dr. D.	All the village now have mated,
	All are happy as can be ;
	I to live alone am fated,
	No one's left to marry me !
Ensemble.	She will tend him, etc.

Exeunt Sir Marmaduke, Mrs. Partlet, Aline *and* Alexis. Dr. Daly *looks after them, then exit.*

Mr. Wells, *who has overheard part of this quintette, and who has remained concealed behind the market cross, comes down as they go off.*

RECITATIVE.—Mr. Wells.

Oh ! I have wrought much evil with my spells,
  An ill I can't undo !
This is too bad of you, J. W. Wells,—
  What wrong have they done you ?
And see, another love-lorn lady comes—
  Alas, poor stricken dame !
A gentle pensiveness her life benumbs,
  And mine alone the blame !

Lady Sangazure *enters.*

Lady S.	Alas ! ah me ! and welladay !
	I sigh for love, and well I may,
	For I am very old and gray.
	But stay !

Sees Mr. Wells, *and becomes fascinated by him.*

RECITATIVE.

Lady S.	What is this fairy form I see before me ?
Mr. W.	Oh horrible ! she's going to adore me !
	This last catastrophe is overpowering !
Lady S.	Why do you glare at one with visage lowering ?
	For pity's sake, recoil not thus from me !
Mr. W.	My lady, leave me—this may never be !

*Duet.—*Lady Sangazure *and* Mr. Wells.

Mr. W.	Hate me ! I drop my H's—have through life !
Lady S.	Love me ! I'll drop them too !
Mr. W.	Hate me ! I always eat peas with a knife !
Lady S.	Love me ! I'll eat like you !
Mr. W.	Hate me ! I spend the day at Rosherville !
Lady S.	Love me ! that joy I'll share !
Mr. W.	Hate me ! I often roll down One-Tree-Hill !
Lady S.	Love me ! I'll join you there !
Lady S.	Love me ! my prejudices I will drop !
Mr. W.	Hate me ! that's not enough !
Lady S.	Love me ! I'll come and help you in the shop !
Mr. W.	Hate me ! the life is rough !
Lady S.	Love me ! my grammar I will all forswear !
Mr. W.	Hate me ! abjure my lot !
Lady S.	Love me ! I'll stick sunflowers in my hair !
Mr. W.	Hate me ! they'll suit you not !

RECITATIVE.—MR. WELLS.

At what I'm going to say be not enraged—
I may not love you, for I am engaged.

LADY S.　Engaged!

MR. W.　　　　　　　　Engaged!
　　　　　To a maiden fair
　　　　　With bright brown hair,
　　　　　　And a sweet and simple smile,
　　　　　Who waits for me
　　　　　By the sounding sea,
　　　　　　On a South Pacific isle.

MR. W.　(*aside.*)　A lie!　No maiden awaits me there!
LADY S.　　　　　　　　　　She has bright brown hair!
MR. W.　(*aside.*)　A lie!　No maiden smiles on me!
LADY S.　　　　　　　　　　By the sounding sea!

ENSEMBLE.

LADY SANGAZURE.	MR. WELLS.
Oh, agony, rage, despair!	Oh, agony, rage, despair!
The maiden has bright brown hair,	Oh, where will this end, oh where?
And mine is white as snow!	I should like very much to know!
False man, it will be your fault,	It will certainly be my fault,
If I go to my family vault	If she goes to her family vault
And bury my life-long woe!	To bury her life-long woe!

BOTH.　　　The family vault—the family vault.

It will certainly be $\left\{ \begin{array}{c} \text{your} \\ \text{my} \end{array} \right\}$ fault,

If $\left\{ \begin{array}{c} \text{I go} \\ \text{she goes} \end{array} \right\}$ to $\left\{ \begin{array}{c} \text{my} \\ \text{her} \end{array} \right\}$ family vault,

To bury $\left\{ \begin{array}{c} \text{my} \\ \text{her} \end{array} \right\}$ life-long woes!

　　　　　　　　　　　　(*Exit* LADY SANGAZURE.)

RECITATIVE.—MR. WELLS.

Oh, hideous doom—to scatter desolation,
　And sow the seeds of sorrow far and wide,
To foster *mésalliances* through the nation,
　And drive high-born old dames to suicide!
Shall I subject myself to reprobation
　By leaving her in solitude to pine?
No! come what may, I'll make her reparation,—
So, aged lady, take me,—I am thine!

　　　　　　　　　　　　(*Exit* MR. WELLS.)

Enter ALINE.

ALINE.　This was to have been the happiest day of my life, but I am very far from happy! Alexis insists that I shall taste the philter, and when I try to persuade him that to do so would be an insult to my pure and lasting love, he tells me that I object because I do not desire that my love for him shall be eternal. Well (*sighing, and producing a phial*), I can at least prove to him that in that he is unjust!

RECITATIVE.

Alexis, doubt me not! My loved one, see,
Thine utter will is sovereign law to me.
All fear, all thought of ill I cast away,—
It is my darling's will, and I obey!
(She drinks the philter.)

The fearful deed is done,
My love is near!
I go to meet my own
In trembling fear.
If o'er us aught of ill
Should cast a shade,
It was my darling's will,
And I obeyed!

As ALINE *is going off, she meets* DR. DALY. *He is playing on a flageolet. Under the influence of the spell she at once becomes strangely
fascinated by him, and exhibits every symptom of being hopelessly in
love with him.*

SONG.—DR. DALY.

Oh, my voice is sad and low,
And with timid step I go,
For with load of love o'erladen
I inquire of every maiden,
"Will you wed me, little lady?
Will you share my cottage shady?"
Little lady answers, "No!
Thank you for your kindly proffer,
Good your heart, and full your coffer;
Yet I must decline your offer—
I'm engaged to so-and so!"
So-and-so!
So-and-so! (*flageolet*)
She's engaged to so-and-so.

What a rogue young hearts to pillage!
What a worker on Love's tillage!
Every maiden in the village
Is engaged to so-and-so!
So-and-so!
So-and so! (*flageolet*)
All engaged to so-and-so!

At the end of the song DR. DALY *sees* ALINE, *and, under the influence
of the potion, falls in love with her.*

ENSEMBLE.—ALINE *and* DR. DALY.

Oh, joyous boon! oh, mad delight!
O sun and moon, O day and night,
Rejoice, rejoice with me!
Proclaim our joy, ye birds above!
Ye brooklets, murmur forth our love
In choral ecstasy!

ALINE.	Oh joyous boon !
DR. D.	Oh, mad delight !
ALINE.	O sun and moon,
DR. D.	O day and night,
BOTH.	Ye birds and brooks and fruitful trees,
	With choral joy delight the breeze,
	Rejoice, rejoice with me !

Enter ALEXIS.

ALEXIS.	Aline, my only love, my happiness !
	The philter—you have tasted it ?
ALINE.	Yes ! yes !
ALEXIS.	Oh, joy ! Mine, mine forever and for aye !

(*Embraces her.*)

ALINE.	Alexis, don't do that—you must not !

(DR. DALY *interposes between them.*)

ALEXIS.	Why ?

DUET.—ALINE *and* DR. DALY.

ALINE.	Alas ! that lovers thus should meet;
	Oh, pity, pity me !
	Oh, charge me not with cold deceit;
	Oh, pity, pity me !
	You bade me drink. With trembling awe
	I drank, and, by the potion's law,
	I loved the very first I saw !
	Oh, pity, pity me !
DR. D.	My dear young friend, consoléd be,
	We pity, pity you.
	In this I'm not an agent free,—
	We pity, pity you.
	Some most extraordinary spell
	O'er us has cast its magic fell ;
	The consequence I need not tell,—
	We pity, pity you.

ENSEMBLE.

Some most extraordinary spell,

O'er { us / them } has cast its magic fell ;

The consequence { we / they } need not tell.

{ We / They } pity, pity { thee ! / me ! }

ALEXIS.	False one, begone ; I spurn thee !
	To thy new lover turn thee !
	Thy perfidy all men shall know.
ALINE.	I could not help it !
ALEXIS.	Come one, come all !
DR. D.	We could not help it !
ALEXIS.	Obey my call !

ALINE.	I could not help it!
ALEXIS.	Come hither—run!
DR. D.	We could not help it!
ALEXIS.	Come, every one!

Enter all the characters except LADY SANGAZURE *and* MR. WELLS.

CHORUS.

Oh, what is the matter, and what is the clatter?
He's glowering at her, and threatens a blow!
Oh, why does he batter the girl he did flatter,
And why does the latter recoil from him so?

RECITATIVE.—ALEXIS.

Prepare for sad surprises,—
My love Aline despises!
No thought of sorrow shames her,
Another lover claims her!
Be his, false girl, for better or for worse,
But, ere you leave me, may a lover's curse—

DR. D. (*coming forward.*) Hold! Be just. This poor child drank the philter at your instance. She hurried off to meet you, but, most unhappily, she met me instead. As you had administered the potion to both of us, the result was inevitable. But fear nothing from me,—I will be no man's rival. I shall quit the country at once, and bury my sorrow in the congenial gloom of a colonial bishopric.

ALEXIS. My excellent old friend! (*taking his hand; then turning to* MR. WELLS, *who has entered with* LADY SANGAZURE.) O Mr. Wells, what, what is to be done?

MR. W. I do not know; and yet there is one means by which this spell may be removed.

ALEXIS. Name it, oh, name it!

MR. W. Or you or I must yield up his life to Ahrimanes. I would rather it were you. I should have no hesitation in sacrificing my own life to spare yours, but we take stock next week, and it would not be fair on the Co.

ALEXIS. True. Well, I am ready!

ALINE. No, no, Alexis, it must not be! Mr. Wells, if he must die that all may be restored to their old loves, what is to become of me? I should be left out in the cold, with no love to be restored to.

MR. W. True, I did not think of that. (*To the others.*) My friends, I appeal to you, and I will leave the decision in your hands.

FINALE.

MR. W.	Or I or he
	Must die!
	Which shall it be?
	Reply!
SIR M.	Die thou!
	Thou art the cause of all offending!
LADY S.	Die thou!
	Yield thou to this decree unbending!
ALL.	Die thou!

MR. W.   So be it ! I submit ! My fate is sealed.
          To popular opinion thus I yield !

(Falls on trap.)

Be happy all, leave me to my despair ;
I go,—it matters not with whom or where !

All quit their present partners and rejoin their old lovers. SIR MAR-
MADUKE *leaves* MRS. PARTLET *and goes to* LADY SANGAZURE.
ALINE *leaves* DR. DALY *and goes to* ALEXIS. DR. DALY *leaves*
ALINE *and goes to* CONSTANCE. NOTARY *leaves* CONSTANCE *and
goes to* MRS. PARTLET. *All the chorus make a corresponding change.*

ALL.

GENTLEMEN.	Oh, my adored one !
LADIES.	Unmingled joy !
GENTLEMEN.	Ecstatic rapture !
LADIES.	Beloved boy !

(They embrace.)

SIR M.   Come to my mansion, all of you ! At least
          We'll crown our rapture with another feast !

SIR MARMADUKE, LADY SANGAZURE, ALEXIS *and* ALINE.

Now to the banquet we press !
Now for the eggs and ham,
Now for the mustard and cress,
Now for the strawberry jam !
CHORUS.   Now to the banquet, etc.

DR. DALY, CONSTANCE, NOTARY, *and* MRS. PARTLET.

Now for the tea of our host,
Now for the rollicking bun,
Now for the muffin and toast, ●
Now for the gay Sally Lunn !
CHORUS.   Now for the tea, etc.

(General dance.)

During the symphony MR. WELLS *sinks through grave trap, amid
red fire.*

FINIS.

CPSIA information can be obtained
at www.ICGtesting.com
Printed in the USA
BVHW041446310719
554800BV00005B/76/P